T0104557

Order this book online at www.trafford.com
or email orders@trafford.com

Most Trafford titles are also available at major online book retailers.

Print information available on the last page.

ISBN: 978-1-4907-7768-9 (sc)
ISBN: 978-1-4907-7770-2 (hc)
ISBN: 978-1-4907-7769-6 (e)

Library of Congress Control Number: 2016918450

Trafford rev. 11/14/2016

 www.trafford.com
North America & international
toll-free: 1 888 232 4444 (USA & Canada)
fax: 812 355 4082

Contents

ABOUT MY BOOK AND ME

I'm an ordinary baby,
Who does what babies can, --
A little blond and curly boy, and born American.

I make my home in Paris,
'Cause it happens we are there,
But I might be <u>any</u> baby, and I <u>might</u> live anywhere!

I've made this book for babies,
And for other people, too, --
About the world, and how it looks from a baby's point of view.

Mummy did the writing part,
But truly I can say,
That I'm the one who made the book, a little every day.

For even though she wrote it down,
It's really mine, you see.
For she didn't write a single thought that didn't <u>start</u> with me.

Oh there is lots of poetry,
In any baby's mind.
When all the world is fresh and new, it's not so hard to find.

Oh there is lots of poetry
That only babies see.
-- Now don't you wish that you could know how a baby sees a
tree?

Or feel with baby feeling
How the morning sunbeams fall?
Or the soft and happy mystery of shadows on the wall?

No grown-up eye can hope to see,
No grown-up heart to know.
You'll have to take it all on faith, because I tell you so.

So I've made this book for babies,
And for their parents, too,
About the world and how it looks from a baby's point of view.

So you and all the others
Can see the things I see,
And understand the thoughts I think, and be good friends
with me.

BALLOON

Up, down,
Up, down,
This is my balloon,
Up, down,
Up, down,
Sing a merry tune,––
Feel it floating up and then
Pull it quickly down again,
Up, down,
Up, down,
This is my balloon.

Up, down,
Up, down,
Sing my little tune,
Up, down,
Up, down,
All the afternoon, ––
It was late when Mummy said,
"Time to put balloon to bed." ––
Up, down,
Up, down,
This is my balloon.

Up, down,
Up, down,
Even in my dreams,
Up, down,
Up, down,
Oh, how strange it seems!
All night long I see it there,
Soft and shiny in the air,
Up, down,
Up, down,
This is my balloon.

Up, Down, up, down, - Balloon

Balloonishly

up, down, up, down, this is my balloon.

up, down, up, down, sing a merry tune.

let it travel up & then pull it quickly down again

up, down, up, down, this is my balloon.

WHEN I GO RIDING ON THE STREET --

When I go riding
On the street,
I love to look
At people's feet.
I love to see
Their funny legs, --
They look like pairs
Of wooden pegs.

I like to look
At horses, too,
And see the things
That autos do.
But most of all
It suits my eye,
To watch the ground
Go slippiing by.

I almost break
My nose to see
The sidewalk slide
Away from me.
What makes it go
So smooth and fast?
What makes it move
As I go past?

This world is full
Of mystery, --
I do not know
Why this should be.
So many things
Are past my ken, --
But there I'm just
Like other men!

BANANAS

I hate this job of being dressed,
It spoils the joy of living.
And washing ears, I call a sin
That's really past forgiving.
Every day I fight a fight,
And <u>sometimes</u> nearly win it. ––
But I can't say <u>much</u> against a world
That has bananas in it.

Folks will not let me carry plates,
Nor wield the little hatchet,
Nor even have my china cup,
To throw it up and catch it.
And why, when Mummy's combed her hair
Won't she let me unpin it?
Still, I can't turn down a world
That has bananas in it.

I have my special sort of cares,
I catch my toe and tumble,
I try to do like acrobats,
And come down feeling humble.
I'm not allowed so many of things
I <u>know</u> should be permitted.
Folks sometimes act as if they thought
That babies come half-witted!
<u>And if to argue's impolite,</u>
<u>Then why do they begin it?</u>
Oh this would be an awful world
Without bananas in it!

Life sometimes seems a pail of tears,
All full of imperfections, ––
Of folks who rush to spoil my plans
From all the four directions, ––
Who hide my horse because, they say,
I don't know how to treat it,
Who leave their candy lying 'round,
Then fuss because I eat it.
I couldn't say with perfect truth
I'm happy every minute,
<u>But why complain about a world</u>
<u>That has bananas in it?</u>

OF COURSE

I had my bucket nearly filled,
My pebbles in a row,
My plans all made when Mother said,
"Come on, it's time to go."

Of course I kicked, of course I yelled, ––
She marched me just the same.
It didn't mean a thing to her
To spoil my lovely game.

I tried that scheme of dragging back,
And getting loose and limp.
A workman looked at me and laughed,
And said I was an imp.

But after we had walked aways,
I had a happy thought
Of milk and bread and apple-sauce
And cookies we had bought.

So I started walking right
Like people ought to do,
Then Mother had to go and meet
A woman that she knew!

They had to stand and talk and talk,
And laugh at silly jokes.
I pulled away at Mother's skirt,
And gave her little pokes.

I had to wait and wait and WAIT!
Of course it made me cross,
When I felt the need of getting home
And eating apple-sauce!

POINT OF VIEW

When I come around in front of you, Mummy, and beg you to
carry me,
It isn't because I'm lazy, it's just that I want to <u>see</u>.

To see the things that are nice, Mummy, you have to be <u>so</u>
tall, —
And 'way down here where <u>I</u> have to walk, it isn't the same
at all.

Nothing can look the same to me as it must look to you.
When I look at a horse, it's only legs, with landscape showing
through!

When I look at a house, it isn't a house, it's just an enormous
wall,
When I look at a house from 'way down here, it isn't a house
at all.

You've been grown up so long, so long, — so long you have
been just <u>you</u>,
You don't remember at all, Mummy, a baby's point of view!

So when I come around in front, and beg you to carry me,
It isn't because I'm lazy, Mummy, it's just that I want to <u>see</u>.

To be up there where you are, Mummy, would be such a
wonderful joy, —
Oh why can't you throw that umbrella away, and carry you
little boy?

BIRTHDAY SONG

Though I am two and only two,

I know what I'm about,
        —— <u>When you have a birthday cake,</u>

        <u>You blow the candles out.</u>

Though I am two and only two,

I know what's right and nice,

        —— <u>You take the biggest knife there is,</u>

        <u>And cut yourself a slice.</u>

Though I am two I know to do

As well as any man,

        —— <u>You tuck your Sunday napkin in,</u>

        <u>And do the best you can.</u>

RAIN AT NIGHT

I heard it raining, raining in the night,
I heard it dropping, dropping from the eaves,
I heard the wind go "Woo –– woo –– woo", and then
I heard the dropping of the rain again,
Among the leaves.
I heard it raining, raining in the night,
I heard it falling, falling from the eaves.

I heard it pitter-patter on the roof,
Like little horses running overhead.
–– I like to hear them running to and fro,
But Teddy-bear gets sort of scared, and so
I have to hold his paw and pat his head.
We hold each other close, and snuggle down
Deep in the bed.
I heard it pitter-patter in the night.
I heard it raining, raining overhead.

THE EGOIST

Along the sunny wall I see
A baby shadow pass,
And a baby's face looks up at me
From the bottom of my glass.

Oh, this must be a baby's world,
For I find them everywhere, --
I even look in Mummy's eyes,
And see a baby there.

WHENEVER MOTHER TAKES A BROOM --

Whenever Mother takes a broom,
I always follow close behind,
And when we clean the living-room,
The lovely, lovely things we find!

Underneath the big divan, --
(It's dark and dusty, too,)
A bit of Sister's silver fan,
Trimmed in blue.

Delightful ends of matches that
I try to strike as best I'm able,
Or maybe stuffings from my cat, --
(The velvet one) -- beneath the table.

Thread the color of my suit,
A button from my daddy's shirt,
A lucious bit of candied fruit
No worse for dirt, --

And yes, those scissors, sharp and bright,
Inside the Morris chair --
I remember <u>now</u> the night
I put them there!

Whenever Mother goes to clean,
I follow close behind,
I doubt if you have ever seen
Things as lovely as we find.

You really couldn't quite believe
The joys uncovered by our broom, --
For I am free to say that we've
A very <u>lived-in</u> living room.

PLAYING GAMES

We like to play at things we do,
And give them funny names,
For life would be most awfully dull
If it weren't for playing games.

Lacing shoes is <u>Poke and Pull</u>, --
It's really lots of fun.
You poke and pull and pull and poke,
And pretty soon they're done.

Putting mittens on is driving
Horses in the stall.
Before you think of getting cross,
You've gone and caught them all.

Oh yes, and climbing into bed
Is getting on a ship.
(Sometimes I'd rather stay at home
Than take <u>that</u> sort of trip!)

We like to play at things we do,
And give them funny names, --
For life would be most awfully dull,
If it weren't for playing games!

BEFORE AND AFTER CHRISTMAS --

Before: I'm tired of these stupid playthings
I've played with all the fall.
Do they really think I can pass my life
With a silly rubber ball?
They try to fool me with a train
That never, never ran.
They think I should be satisfied
With a talcum powder can!

After: Of course I liked my Christmas tree,
And all the pretty things. --
They gave me really, truly cars,
And aeroplanes with wings.
But now I'm tired of the wind-up train,
And the foolish dancing man,
And I want to go in my room and play
With the talcum powder can!

Once when I was very hot,
On an August afternoon,
Daddy took me on his lap,
And made a little tune:

> "Oh, he's hot, hot, hot,
> Little tot, tot, tot, ––
> He's a hottentot, a hottentot,
> A hotten––, hotten––, hottentot."

Daddy jogged me on his knee,
And sang his little song,
Then Sister brought a pan and spoon,
And played them like a gong:

> "Oh, he's hot, hot, hot,
> Little tot, tot, tot, ––
> He's a hottentot, a hottentot,
> A hotten––, hotten––, hottentot."

When Mummy came and saw the fun,
She got down on her knees,
And clapped her hands in measure, like
The ab-or-ige-nes.

> "Oh, he's hot, hot, hot,
> Little tot, tot, tot, ––
> He's a hottentot, a hottentot,
> A hotten––, hotten––, hottentot."

Family Jazz

With Warm Feeling

Oh he's hot-hot-hot-little -tot-tot-tot, he's a

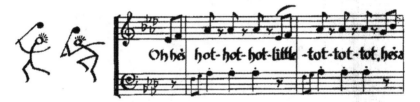

hottentot, a hottentot, a hotten-hotten-hottentot.

Oh he's hot-hot-hot-little -tot-tot-tot, he's a

hottentot, a hottentot, a hotten-hotten-hottentot.

Family Jazz   (contd.)

Oh he's hot- hot- hot-little -tot-tot-tot, he's a

hottentot, a hottentot, a hotten-hotten-hottentot.

Hotten- -totter

Much- -hotter

Hot

G.S.F.

I CAN'T GO TO BED --

I can't go to bed till I find those blocks,
Now can I, Daddy?
I have to be sure that they're safe in the box,
Now don't I, Daddy?
To know that there're two of them wandering wild
Would bother 'most <u>any</u> orderly child.
I <u>must</u> have them in all neatly piled,
Now mustn't I Daddy?

I think that is one of them under the bed, --
Do you see it, Daddy?
Perhaps I can reach it. -- I'll stand on my head
If you'll help me, Daddy.
-- Now Mummy is calling, and saying it's late,
Oh Daddy, explain why we're making her wait. --
We can't go to bed till we find those blocks,
Now can we, Daddy?

First the red leaves fall, and then the yellow, ––
Then the brown ones crumple up, and follow.

Last, from some tall tree that grows so high
You cannot see its branches through the sky.

A cloud of soft, white leaves comes floating down
To cover up the red ones and the brown.

Such tiny, funny, chilly leaves they are!
One hits my coat, and leaves a baby star.

They give me small, cold kisses on the nose,
And go away again, where no one knows.

THE BABY'S HOUSE

I want a house with a garden, --
With a garden full of trees,
With the trees all full of blossoms,
And the blossoms full of bees.

I want a house with an attic,
As big as it can be,
So when my little brother comes
He can play up there with me.

I want a house near Grandma's,
So I can feel she's near, --
So I can climb on my grandpa's knee,
And whisper in his ear.

Oh, it will be nice in the garden, --
All shady beneath the trees.
I'll smell of all the blossoms,
And talk with all the bees.

And if I could manage to coax inside
A little, ripply stream,
It would be the really, truly house
That is every baby's dream

IT'S ONLY NICE RAIN, MUMMY --

It's only nice rain, Mummy,
That's coming down.
Oh why don't we go out in it?
I'd love to walk about in it
Around the town.
It's only nice rain, Mummy,
That's coming down.

It's really very nice rain, Mummy,
All soft and wet.
Oh let me put my slicker on, --
A sweater or something thicker on, --
It's early yet.
And it's only the very nicest sort of rain,
All soft and wet.

Can't you believe that it is nice rain, Mummy,
When I tell you so?
Look, the neighbor's maid is out in it,
She looks so comfy and so stout in it, --
So pleased to go.
If it weren't the nicest kind of nice rain, Mummy,
Would I tell you so?

All right, I s'pose I'll have to play inside then, Mummy,
But if I pout,
Remember it's a disappointed boy
Who can't go out.
And 'course you understand how it must grieve me,
To have a mother who will not believe me.
Now don't you hear how nice that rain sounds, Mummy,
In the spout?.

WHEN I WAS A LITTLE BABY --

When I was a little baby
On a pillow, kitten-wise,
My mother leaned above me,
And smiled into my eyes.

When I was a little older,
Mother and Daddy too,
Smiled at me together
Like loving parents do.

But lately those silly grown-ups
have taken another tack, --
Now they smile at each other,
Behind my back!

BALCONY

If I should take a chair
Out on the balcony,
And climb out into the air,
Where would I be?

Daddy heard me thinking about it,
And locked the door.

They won't let me out on the
balcony
Anymore.

ROUNDALAY

Round and round and round and round,
Round and round the table, ––
Fifteen, twenty, thirty times,
Forty if I'm able.
After I'm at thirty-five,
Things sort of change, you see, ––
The furniture starts going round
Instead of me.

SISTER'S CATS

On winter days, toward half past four,
I go and scratch at Sister's door.
For there is always hope that she
Might come and draw some cats for me.

The cats she draws are something grand,
She takes a pencil in her hand,
And on the paper there appears
The startings of a pair of ears.

A line or two, and here they come, —
The back and tail and tumy-tum.
Those two small dots we know are eyes,
Those four short lines look whisker-wise.

The ones that play and run at rats
Don't look at all like Sister's cats, —
But all the same, hers seem to me
As nice as any cats could be.

And sometimes when the window glass
Is misty from the fogs that pass,
She draws them there, so big and tall, —
The most enchanting cats of all!

Sister's Cats

Mummy Cat

PEEKABOO, MOON

Peekaboo, Moon, behind the cloud,
There, I see you sliding!
Don't you think that I know, you Moon,
Exactly where you're hiding?
If you thought I was fooled,
Why you thought too soon,
Peekaboo, Moon!

Peekaboo, Moon, behind the tree,
Where the little wind is blowing,
Don't you think that I know, you Moon,
Exactly where you're going?
I'll wait right here
If you hide till noon,
Peekaboo, Moon!

PRIDE AFTER A FALL

I skinned my leg,
And how it bled!
It made the clean
White hanky red.
At first it smarted
Pretty bad,
But oh I'm proud,
And oh I'm glad.
For of all the things
A boy enjoys, ––
It's showing a "hurt"
To the other boys.
And all tied up
Above my sock
I'll be the hero
Of the block.

AND SISTER MADE THIS ONE --

No longer a baby, and not yet a boy, --

What shall we call him? -- He's only a toy.

THE DOOR OF THE SKY --

The door of the sky
Is covered with clouds,
So nobody ever can find it, ––

But oh I know
There's a lovely house
With a garden of stars, behind it.

GOOSEBERRIES

Oh Mummy and I work together so well,
When there're berries to stem and there're stories to tell.

We pour them all out on the table and then
Pretend that they're geese to be chased in a pen.

Or else that they're salmon or minnows or whales,
And we pick off their heads and pick of their tails.

Oh Mummy and I work together so well
When there're berries to stem and there're stories to tell!

TWINS

He looks all smily as I pass,
The nicest boy lives in the glass, --
And I would be so glad if he
Would hop outside and play with me.

The meanest boy lives in there, too.
He scowls and looks me through and through.
His frowns are terrible to see, --
I hope he doesn't look like <u>me</u>!

HI, DIDDLE, DIDDLE

Hi, diddle, diddle, the cat and the fiddle,
The cow jumped over the moon, --
The little dog laughed to see such sport,
And the dish ran away with the spoon.

Hi, diddle, diddle, the cat and the fiddle,
The cow jumped oh so high, --
Whenever we're able, while sitting at table,
We play it, my daddy and I!

Hi, diddle, diddle, the cat and the fiddle,
This is a merry life, --
The cat is a cup with the milk drunk up, --
The fiddle, the butter knife!

Hi, diddle, diddle, the cat and the fiddle,
Now would you ever dream
The little dog who laughed so hard
Was the pitcher that held the cream?

Hi, diddle, diddle, the cat and the fiddle,
What more could a body wish?
The spoon is <u>my</u> spoon, that matches the moon --
The dish, it is just a dish.

Hi, diddle, diddle, the cat and the fiddle,
This is the joke we play, --
When Mummy comes for the dish and spoon,
Why, both of them run away!

Hi, diddle, diddle, the cat and the fiddle,
The cow jumped oh so high, --
Whenever we're able, while sitting at table,
We play it, my daddy and I!

Hi, diddle, diddle

Diddlishly

Hi, diddle, diddle, the cat & the fiddle, the cow jumped oh, so high, when-ever we're able, while sitting at table, we play it my daddy & I

MOON -- à la moderne

Mother, I want to see the moon,
What made them turn it off so soon?

It starts nice thinkings in my head,
To see it as I climb in bed.

Just to know it's shining there,
Fastened to its roof of air,

Gives me pleasant thoughts to keep
Me company when I'm asleep.

Please, I would like to see the moon.
What made them turn it off so soon?

Mother, go tell those electric men
I wish they'd turn it on again!

OH MOON THAT HANGS ON THE AIRY WALL --

Oh moon that hangs
On the airy wall,
What holds you there
So you don't fall?
What makes your light, so soft and white, --
Oh moon, who put you there at all?

And what far land
Do you shine on
When daylight comes,
And night is gone?
Do you go to bed, or shine ahead, --
Oh what becomes of you at dawn?

There's lots of stars, --
Oh quite a few,
Perhaps a hundred,
Maybe two.
That's why, you see, you int'rust me,
Because there's only <u>one</u> of you.

Oh moon that hangs
On the airy wall,
What holds you there
So you don't fall?
When I can look in a grown up book,
I 'spose I'll learn about it all.

But now that I'm
Not more than three,
I'll have to let
Those hard things be, ––
And while I wait to grow to eight,
Oh moon, dear moon, be friends with me!

ABOUT THE MOON

Oh now I know
About the moon,
And this is how
I came to know.
I had a blue
And gray balloon,
The wind came by, --
I let it go.
The wind came by
And lifted up
The gray balloon
Above the trees,
And shining like
A silver cup
It rode away
Upon the breeze.
It tried to turn
To earth, and then
The wind ran up
And pushed it higher,
I saw it dip
And rise again,
And pass beyond
The tallest spire.

Now don't you see
About the moon,
And why it hangs
Upon the air?
Once it was
A white balloon
That left the earth

And wandered there.
It must have gone
Beyone the trees,
Beyond the clouds,
And near a star.
Away across
The airy seas,
To where some other
Children are.
"Oh see," they cried,
Here in the sky,
The lovely ball
So smooth and white.
Now all day long
They let it fly,
But tie it to
A cloud at night.

So now I know,
About the moon, --
Some baby lost it
Long ago.
I lost my blue
And gray balloon,
And that is how
I came to know.

THE MOON--STEALER

I saw the moon the other night. --
It made me start to think
Of such a grand and simple scheme,
I couldn't sleep a wink.

Why not go and steal that moon
Some night when it is new?
I've thought out every move to make,
And this is what I'll do:

First, I'll climb the Eiffel Tower,
And when I've reached the top,
I'll jump into an aeroplane
That I have told to stop.

And when we've travelled up and up
To where the planets are,
I'll tell the driver he can go,
And step from star to star.

I'll walk till I can reach the moon,
And touch it with my thumb, --
Then I'll stand on my two tip-toes,
And pick it like a plum.

Then I'll choose the softest cloud
That's sort of lying 'round,
And ride it gently down until
My feet can touch the ground.

And there I'll be at my own front door,
As neat as any pin.
(Of course I thought to take the key,
Else how could I get in?)

And being careful not to drop
The shiny, pretty moon,
I'll hide it in the side-board drawer
With my solid silver spoon.

Then I'll crawl in bed so still
They'll never know that I
Was out alone, and stealing moons,
And riding in the sky.

Then when Mummy wakes me up
By kissing both my eyes,
<u>I'll take her in the dining-room,</u>
<u>And show her the surprise</u>!

A-crossing the Atlantic

SEA DREAMS

A-crossing the Atlantic ––

I think it's lots of fun to be
A-crossing the Atlantic.
The stewards come and talk to me,
And bring me funny things to see.
We sleep in bunks <u>so</u> cosily,
A-crossing the Atlantic.

The waiter always comes before
We're up, and waits outside the door.
He says: "We'd be so pleased to bring
You almost any sort of thing,
Sole or lobster à la king.
Simply tell us what to do, ––
You know the boat belongs to you,
A-crossing the Atlantic."

Then Mother says: "Well we'd enjoy
A little spinich for the boy.
All mashed up and not too cold.
A very little's all he'll hold, ––
For he is not so very old,
A-crossing the Atlantic.

And then they bring, upon my soul,
A ton of spinach in a bowl.
<u>We throw it out the big port-hole</u>
<u>Right into the Atlantic!</u>
(I hope the little baby fish
Feel kindly toward that special dish, ––
They must have all the weeds they wish,
Out there in the Atlantic.)

Once when we were out on deck,
A-crossing the Atlantic,
We saw a little tiny speck,
Just like a duck without a neck,
A-crossing the Atlantic.
Sister said: "There goes a ship,
That's out like we are, for a trip
Across the big Atlantic."

"What," I thought, "a little boat
As small as that can keep afloat
Upon the big Atlantic?"
Then Daddy went and got his glass,
So I could see that boatie pass,
And my, but it was big and tall,
And not a baby boat at all,
Astray on the Atlantic.

I like to think that other ships
Are sailing on the sea,
And other babies taking trips
To Europe, just like me.
It's nice to know that another boat
Sails along and keeps afloat
Upon the big Atlantic.
For it is very lonely on
The ocean, when the sun is gone.

Sometimes, when it's late at night
Upon the big Atlantic,
The winds and waves begin to fight,
And screech and howl and try to bite,
And I am just a tiny mite
A-crossing the Atlantic.
Then my daddy holds my hand,

And says we're warm and cozy, and
As safe as if we were on land,
And <u>not</u> on the Atlantic.
He tells me how the little bell,
Rings to say that all is well,
That all is well
And all is well,
A-crossing the Atlantic.

So I don't care how the winds may blow,
Or the big brass whistles call,
And when I snuggle down to sleep,
I'm not afraid at all,
For even if the water's deep,
He'll see that I don't fall.
And it is simply marvellous
To dream the boat belongs to us, —
It moves without a bit of fuss
Across the big Atlantic.

For Daddy is the pilot, who
Decides which winds shall blow,
And Mummy is the engineer,
Who makes the engines go.
And I'm the captain, all in blue,
Who calls out, "Fast!" and "Slow!"
And sister rings the little bell,
To let us know that all is well,
That all is well,
And all is well,
A-crossing the Atlantic.

Passing Land's End --

Daddy put on my woolly coat
And carried me out on deck;
It was a dark as dark as dark could be,
And I held on tight to his neck

All we could see was the pilot's light,
And the funnels in a row,
All we could hear was the water,
Talking down below.

There wasn't a moon or even a star
To see the ocean by,
But just one speck of light
That twinkled like an eye.

It bobbed up and down on the water
And it seemed to wink at me
Like a little Christmas candle
That had fallen in the sea.

It might have been a baby star
That had tumbled down the stair, --
But Daddy said: "Do you see that light?
That's England over there.

And over there in England
There are boys with wooly coats.
They put on caps when they go outside,
And mufflers around their throats.

They take off their shoes by an open fire
As pleasant as can be.
They eat their supper at half past four,
Only there they call it <u>tea</u>.

They play in fields all green with grass
With flocks of wooly sheep,
And the little girls make daisy-chains,
And take them home to keep.

England's the land of currant buns,
And ships that sail the seas,
And Kings and Queens in crowns of gold,
And blossoming hawthorne trees.

And now I think that we'll go downstairs,
"For it's late," my Daddy said,
"And I'm sure that those English babies
Have long since gone to bed."

I wanted to tell my mother
About those woolly sheep,
And how the King eats currant buns
Before he goes to sleep.

But oh the way seemed dark and long,
And half way down the stair,
I began to dream of England
And the people living there.

They gave me a cup of cambric tea,
And then they began to sing
A funny song that was awf'lly long,
And all about the King!

They gave me a great big currant bun
To put beneath my head, ––
They brought me a little wooly lamb,
And tucked us both in bed.

And when we'd settled down to sleep
Cozilly through the night,
The Queen in a golden apron
Came and turned out the light.

Sea Lullaby --

Big ship,
Strong ship,
Carry the baby far,
Over the singing, swinging waves,
Out where the islands are,
Out where the smoke of the big smoke stack
Goes oozing out all woozy black,
And curling around a star,
Curling around a star.

Big ship,
Strong ship,
Sail on the fishy deep,
Over the curling, swirling waves,
Out where the dolphins leap.
Where the big sea serpent swings his tail,
And the porpoise plays with the baby whale,
And the moon comes down to take a sail
While the baby lies asleep,
While the baby lies asleep.

Big ship,
Strong ship,
Carry the baby home.
Over the gleaming, dreaming waves,
Over the crests of foam.
Into the shore, the happy shore,
Into the port, the port once more,
Safe inside of my Daddy's door,
Carry the baby home,
Carry the baby home.

DICTIONARIES

I love to take the big books
Down off the shelf.
I like encyclopedias
To look at by myself.

They're full of lovely pictures, ––
I wish that they were mine.
–– Bother, here is Sister,
And she says, "Nein!"

I guess if she were really mad
She wouldn't use her Dutch, ––
(Sister studies German,
Though her grammar isn't much.)

Now that she has left me,
I'll have another look.
Maybe there is something nice
In <u>that</u> big book.

Oh what a pretty one,
Standing all alone.
–– Bother, here is Mother,
And she says, "Non!"

No need to pay attention,
Although I understood, ––
(Mother knows Italian,
Though her accent isn't good.)

Now here's Daddy coming,
I hear him saying, "Net!"
(Daddy's learning Russian,
but he hasn't finished yet.)

Oh but <u>that's</u> a lovely book,
Standing 'way up there!
Maybe I can get it down,
By standing on a chair.

–– No, I guess I'd better not,
The time has come to go.
<u>For they're all descending on me</u>
<u>With a good old English NO</u>!

DADDY GOES AWAY

Daddy explains ––

> Daddy said, "My little son,
> I have to go away
> To make some money to buy your milk,
> And games for you to play."
>
> I couldn't find a single word
> All comforty and nice,
> So I put my arms around his neck
> And kissed my daddy twice.

Gray dawn ––

> It was very early morning, and so dark you couldn't
> see, ––
> I winked and blinked and rubbed my eyes when
> Mummy wakened me.
> I winked and blinked and rubbed some more, ––
> what <u>could</u> the trouble be?
>
> I sighed a great big gusty sigh, and snuggled down
> in bed,
> And burrowed till the pillows almost covered up my
> head.
> "But we have to go with Daddy to the station," ––
> Mummy said.

"It can't be more than five o'clock," I heard my
sister say,
"An awful hour, an awful train, an awful rainy day.
An awful feeling all around when Daddy goes away."

I sat up then and listened, and I felt an awful fear.
How can I let my daddy go, and stay for 'most a year?
Whatever will the house be like when Daddy isn't
here?

I couldn't eat my cereal, –– (I hate it, anyway) ––
Daddy stirred his coffee fast, and hadn't much to say.
How strange the breakfast tasted when my daddy
went away!

When we got to the station, –– that is Saint Lazare,
you know, ––
The engine gave puff and jerk, and whistled sort
of low.
I thought it sounded sorry, too, 'cause Daddy had
to go.

Daddy kissed us twice around, and thumped me on
the head.
"I'll get my nice new handky out to wave good-by,"
he said.
But when the train began to move, he wiped his
eyes, instead.

Daddy comes back --

Mummy is happy,
And Sister is gay,
For Daddy, my Daddy
Is coming today.

Sister is dressed
In her shiny new clothes
And Mummy is careful
To powder her nose.

We jump in a taxi
Because we can't wait,
And say to the driver,
"Please hurry, we're late!"

Then we get to the station,
And wait in the rain
Because it's an hour
Till it's time for the train.

It seems like a day
That we're waiting, to me,
The hands of the clock
Are as still as can be.

It's <u>hundreds</u> of hours
Since we got here, I know, --
Oh Daddy, my Daddy,
Your train is so slow!

–– Then a toot in the distance,
Blue porters in line.
Now the nice little shivers
Play tag up my spine!

Sister looks pleased
In her shiny new clothes,
And Mummy is careful
To powder hor nose.

A bell and a whistle,
A light on the track, ––
Oh Daddy, my Daddy
I'm <u>glad</u> you are back!

WINTER WALK

Down by the river, the river we go,
Oh it's beautiful winter weather,
With a bit of wind and a bit of snow,
And the sunshine all together!

Here there are boats, there are boats to see,
Heavy with coal and sand,
Barges that pass so lazily
I could touch them with my hand.

They move like sleepy horses do,
And the water is so calm
They pass with never a ripple through
The shadow of Notre Dame.

Down by the river, the river we go, --
(Oh the Eiffel Tower is high!)
We wait sometimes till the sun is low,
And never a boat comes by.

Sometimes we wait till it's really night,
And never a boat we see, --
Till the Eiffel Tower is a blaze of light,
Like a giant Christmas tree.

THE FIRST INTERNATIONAL

We run and play together,
We children in the park.
Rosette was born in Italy, ––
That's why her curls are dark.

Pierre's a little Frenchman,
He wears a pinafore.
His sister's name is Jeanne-Marie,
Their papa keeps a store.

Malouska is a Russian,
But she's come to France to stay.
(They had a Revolution,
And <u>her</u> papa got away.)

We run and play together,
We children in the park.
Our mamas knit, or merely sit,
Until it's nearly dark.

We take each other's buckets,
We use each other's balls,
And Pierre is very sorry,
When Maloushka falls

Once we had an awful time,
I really can't say why.
I grabbed a shovel,
Rosette began to cry.

Jeanne had a tantrum
And pulled up the grass, ––
Maloushka hit Pierre because
He wouldn't let her pass.

Jeanne-Marie was madder yet,
And looked an awful way,
And told Maloushka she could go
To Leningrad and stay.

Mother got my ball and spade,
And made <u>me</u> come along.
She said it was no place for us!
The fight was going strong.

Going home, she told me twice
How it was up to me
To show them all how very nice
<u>Americans</u> can be!

OPTIMISTS

They seem to lead a busy life,
Those fishers on the Seine.
They throw their lines into the water,
And pull them out again.

They hang their hooks with little worms
As often as the wish.
And once about a year ago,
I saw one catch a fish.

CHAMPS DE MARS

The Champs de Mars is lovely
On a sunny April day.
It's full of little children
Who come to run and play.
And they're all dressed up in pink and blue,
In the nicest sort of way.

All around the fountain
Their nurse-mades sit and chat.
They sometimes stop to look around,
And see what the babies are at,
And each one wears a starchy cap,
And an apron ironed out flat.

Mummy and I don't seem to have
That silk-and-satiny look.
Mummy never wears a cap,
And she always carries a book.
My coat is sort of thick and blue,
And lined inside with red.
And I wear a little blue beret,
That sits on the side of my head, --
When I'd like a suit all gray and rose
And trimmed in fur, instead.

Once I suggested to Mummy,
It might be well, perhaps,
For her to go buy her an apron,
And a couple of pretty caps, --
So when we walk in the Champs de Mars
When the sky is clear and blue,
She'd look all starched and proper,
Like those other nurse-maids do.
But I somehow felt she didn't get the proper point of view.

She seemed to take it as a joke,
And it wasn't that at all.
She looked at me with that laughy look
They give you when you're small.
I stood upon my dignity,
And asked her to get my ball.
Then she sat down on a bench
Some laughter to enjoy,
And said: "<u>You've high-toned notions for a poor professor's boy</u>!"

MAY PICNIC

The train stood still
Till we go out, ––
I took one long look
All about.
I stood and took
One long, long look, ––
It was springtime all about!

    Oh, Mummy, here is everything, ––
    Oh, Mummy, we have found the spring!

The red, red roofs among the trees, ––
The white road running off down hill,
A little breeze
To play and tease,
A little breeze that won't stay still, ––
A flowering hedge,
An old stone bridge,
A little stream to turn the mill,
The little birds that peep and call,
And the sunshine shining on it all.

We pass the schoolhouse with the well,
And the old stone church with the hung-up bell.
We had some baskets full of lunch,
And little choc'late bars to munch.
And Sister said: "I even think
That we can find him milk to drink."

    Oh, Mummy, here is everything, ––
    Oh, Mummy, we have found the spring!

The ploughed-up fields lay all around
As brown as they could be,
We crossed them all
And climbed a wall
To get the milk for me.
And there was the house, and there was the barn,
And there was the apple tree!
There was the dog,
And there was the cat,
And there was the speckled goat.
There was the hair on his funny chin,
And the collar around his throat.
There was the family of ducks,
And the pond for them to float.

Oh, Mummy, here is everything, ––
Oh, Mummy, we have found the spring!

All day long
The warm sun shone,
And our feet got used to the ground.
Our feet got used to the hmped-up ground,
And Sister said: "It's got so now
It seems quite right to see a cow,
When you stop to look around."

I lay on my tummy beside the brook,
To watch the ripples pass,
A "creeked" my neck to see why clouds
Make shadows on the grass.
And Mummy had to comb her hair
Without a looking-glass!

I took my nap
Beneath a tree,
The wind sang little
Songs to me.
When I woke up
We'd cake for tea.
And Sister took me where I could
Pick daisies in a little wood.

The pleasant day went on and on,
Till all of a sudden it was gone,
"We're going now,
But we'll come again,
So pick you some daisies
To take in the train."

Oh, Mummy, here is everything, —
Oh, Mummy, must we leave the spring?
I fell so queer in my tummy there,
When something's gone, and I don't know where!

As we climbed the long, white-ribbony road,
We passed some oxen with a load,
The driver nodded with his head.
"We are going to get some rain," he said.
The birds were peeping and cheeping low,
And the oxen plugged along, so slow,
— The little bells that the white sheep wear,
And the big old bell in the steeple there,
Were shaking their music into the air.
And like an echo
Answering back,
We heard the train bell,
Down the track.

Near Paris, it began to rain,
I dropped my choc'late, which I love.
I left my daisies in the train,
Sister lost her right-hand glove,
The sky was thick just like a wall,
You'd never know it was spring at all.

But anyway, since we were out
That day, to find the spring,
I know what spring is all about
As well as anything.
Now I know where the country is,
In the stories Mummy tells, ––
Now I know how water tastes,
When it's drawn from mossy wells,
Now I know how the evening sounds
When it's full of little bells,
Oh now I know
Where the daisies grow,
And how the spring-time smells!

And it's a pleasant thought to me,
to know it's spring in Normandy!

Finding the Spring

there was a speckled Goat

and a family of Duck.

FLAGS

I think a flag's a lovely thing, ––
Its colors rise and dip,
A-streaming out against the wind,
Or riding with a ship.

The Dutch flag's a sturdy flag,
Of blue and white and red.
You know the ship's a steady ship,
When it is overhead.

'Most any flag that tops a mast
Will make a splendid sight, ––
But my flag's a special flag,
That's taken in at night.

The British lion's brave and fierce;
He seems to like it there,
A-lying flat upon his neck
And clawing at the air.

The flag of Italy is bright,
The flag of Spain is gay, ––
But my flag is full of stripes
That run the other way.

The tricolor's a merry sight
When riding brave and high, ––
But my flag's a starry flag,
That blows against the sky.

GRANDPA'S TOWN

My mother tells me often
How we'll go to Grandpa's Town, ––
We'll hurry to the station
In a taxi green and brown.

We'll take a train and then a ship,
And then another train.
We'll pass through towns and forests,
And waving fields of grain.

We'll cross the Rocky Mountains,
But before we reach the sea,
We'll find that we are getting close
To where we want to be.

And after days of travelling
We'll take the suit-case down.
The ticket man will come and say,
"All out for Grandpa's Town!"

My heart will beat most awf'lly fast;
I'll hold to Mummy's hand,
Whoever's been to Grandpa's Town
Will surely understand.

For when you've sat for days and days
And watched the towns go past,
<u>You scarcely can believe it,</u>
<u>When you get some place at last</u>.

Grandpa will be waiting there,
And Grandma too, I know,
And all the smiling aunties,
A-standing in a row.

I 'spose I'll hold a little back,
Because I'm only three,
And it makes me feel so awf'lly queer
When people stare at me.

But when I see my grandpa's face,
All shiny like a star,
I'll put my arms around his neck,
And say, "Well, here we are!"

Oh, Paris is so very dear,
It makes me feel most awf'lly queer
Though why I couldn't say,
To think of Paris staying here,
(For Paris is so very dear!)
While I sail far away.

TOURIST

Of course I know New York.
We went to a hotel to stay,
And on my window-sill each day,
A little sparrow came to call.
There wasn't much of him at all;
His tail was like a pickle-fork.
Of course, I know New York!

Why yes, I know Madrid.
It was hot upon the street,
And in the houses, there was heat.
'Twas there I lost my new straw hat.
You can't forget a thing like that!
We never found where it was hid,
Why yes, I know Madrid!

Sure, I know London town.
Mummy went to buy a coat.
Daddy took a check and wrote.
The coat was the nicest I ever have seen,
Soft and warm, and all lined with green.
The collar was big, and furry, and brown.
Sure, I know London town!

FIREWORKS

We went to see the fireworks
On the Fourteenth of July, ––
They had them down by the river,
And they shot them off in the sky.
And the night was dark and the bridges were dark,
And the river was flowing by.

They started late, oh awf'lly late,
And it was aggravating.
The river went on flowing by,
And the people went on waiting.
"Now when they say they'll start at ten,
Why must it be eleven?" ––
I asked my mother forty times,
And my daddy forty –– seven.

Then all of a sudden came a shout,
And there were the fireworks, starting out.
First, it was a silver boat,
And next it was a flower,
And then a bursting ball of light
That shot away into the night,
Beyond the Eiffel Tower.
And now a rocket,
Climbing higher,
And now a star
Above the spire.
And now a river all afire,
A-running down the sky.
Then a shower of shiny rain,
And then the sky all dark again.

We went to see the fireworks
On the Fourteenth of July,
They had them down by the river,
And they shot them off in the sky.
"And waiting one whole year for more's
Most awf'lly hard," said I.
—— Now, in my sleep 'most every night,
I see them once again.
The baskets full of shiney flowers,
The gold and silver rain.
And when I roll and talk and groan, it's not that I've a pain,
It's fireworks, fireworks, fireworks,
A-shooting in my brain.

WHEELS

There are wheels on the auto,
And wheels on the train,
And wheels on the windmill
That stands on the plain.
The wheels in the ships
Make them move on their keels,
And the ships in the air
Have their fast-turning wheels.
The wheels of the fish
Are the queerest of things,
The wheels of the bird
People speak of as wings.
Babies can't walk
'Cause their wheels are too small,
And flowers that don't have them
Can't travel at all.
Sometimes I hear
When it's starry and white,
The wheels of the earth
As it turns in the night.
Oh, how funny and twirly and whirly it feels
To live in a world that is run upon wheels!

JOOBER

"Joober this and Joober that,
And Joober killed a yellow cat,"
Joober took a gun and shot,
Now the yellow cat is <u>not</u>.
Joober this and Joober that,
And Joober killed a yellow cat,
–– Yellow kitty with his claws,
Fought and scratched and broke the laws.
Joober said, "It doesn't pay
For cats to carry on <u>that</u> way,
<u>I</u> will settle him," –– and that
Is how he killed the yellow cat.
Joober this and Joober that,
Joober whittled as he sat,
Joober said, "It takes some nerve
To give those cats what they deserve.
Joober this and Joober that,
And Joober killed a yellow cat.

Yellow cat had lots of fun
Catching mice upon the run,
Catching birds upon the fly,
Catching fish to let them dry.
Joober said, "At night he creeps
While the fam'ly lies and sleeps,
'Cross the roofs all slick with rain,
<u>Busts in through the window pane</u>!
<u>And when he finds a boy in bed</u>
<u>Claws him up</u>!" –– so Joober said.
Joober this and Joober that,
And Joober killed a yellow cat.

Joober said, "Just watch his eyes,
He's the <u>devil</u> in disguise."
–– When it's night, I'm glad he's gone,
Glad he's not upon the lawn,
Glad he's not beside my bed, ––
Glad the yellow cat is dead.
But I get to wond'ring when
Daylight comes around again,
Maybe Joober thought that he
Was <u>smart</u> to be a-spoofing me.

Maybe kitty's heart was good, ––
Maybe no one understood, ––
Maybe he was rather nice, ––
Meant no harm by catching mice.
He was wicked and all that,
Still, he was a kitty-cat.
Joober this and Joober that,
And Joober killed a yellow cat.
Joober this and Joob' the other,
I'm glad Joober's not <u>my</u> brother.

AUTOMOBILE

The wheels of the auto
Go 'round as they ought, oh!
Around and around and around, ––
Around and around
With a whirrity sound, ––
The wonderful wheels of the auto.

Now that is a wonderful thought, oh!
I thought while observing the auto,
When the wheels go around
With a whirrity sound,
Now <u>what</u> makes the auto get over the ground?
The wonderful, wonderful auto!

I like to pretend that we bought, oh!
A whirrity, scurrity auto,
With fenders all shiney,
And buttons so tiny,
All over the seat of the auto.
But I guess we'll not buy it this morning,
So what is the use of forlorning?
I've got a penny,
But Daddy's not any,
And so we're not buying an auto.

But I still have my wonderful thought, oh!
I thought while observing the auto.
The wheels go around
With a whirrity sound
<u>And away down the road goes the auto</u>!

TELEPHONE

It's lots of fun to be alone
While Mummy's at the telephone.

To get the painted dishes out,
And pile them neatly all about.

To ravel out the sewing silk,
And help the kitty drink his milk.

Whenever someone gives a ring,
I'm just as pleased as anything.

One whole half hour to snoop and climb, ––
Be certain I improve the time!

One whole half hour (and often more)
To pile the books upon the floor.

One whole half hour to risk my head,
One whole half hour for jam, (no bread).

One whole half hour to call my own,
While Mummy's at the telephone!

ELEVATOR

Up, up, elevator,
Elevator, up!
First floor gliding by,
Second floor sliding by,
Third floor we go riding by, ––
Elevator, up!
Fourth floor slipping past,
See the numbers tripping past,
Now don't you go to tipping as
You go up and up!

If, instead of stopping at the roof,
We just went climbing on into the sky,
Why, we could touch the stars in broad daylight,
And the white clouds floating by.
And maybe if we looked with all our eyes,
Upon some bright, clear-seeing summer day,
Why, we might even see my grandma's house,
A thousand miles away.

Down, down, elevator,
Elavator, down!
We are going for a walk
All around the town.
Fifth floor gliding by,
Fourth floor sliding by,
Third floor we go riding by,
Elevator, down!
Now the walls are moving fast,
Now the second floor is past,
Now we get to earth at last, ––
Elevator, down!

If, instead of stopping at the floor,
We went on slipping deep into the ground,
I wounder, would we find those little men
Like boys in books have found?
The brownies and the kobalds and the gnomes
That have such clever hands and nimble feet, --
Who knows but what perhaps they make their homes
Below OUR street?

THE SONG OF THE TRAIN

Over the prairie,
Over the plain,
Here me calling,
I am the train.
Across the river,
Along the shore,
Oh for a hundred
Miles or more,
Into the tunnel,
Out again
Hear me coming, --
I am the train.
Around the mountain,
Circling back,
Hear me thunder
Along the track!
Into the city, --
Beware, I say!
Hear my whistle,
And clear the way!
My voice is a knife
That cuts the sky,
As I greet my brother-train,
Passing by.
I fill the air
With a smoky stain,
Hail, all hail
To the conquering train!
Into the city,
Out again,
Into the country,
Over the plain.
Over the prairie,
Far away

Where shall I be
At the break of day? ––
Softly sounds
Through the falling rain,
The faint, small voice
Of the distant train.
Far oh far
On the river shore,
Faint, oh faint
It calls once more,
Even the echoes
Cease at last,
All is still,
For the train has passed!

TOOTHACHE TALES

When drinks and pats and loving words,
And Proper Methods fail, ––
Mummy takes me in her bed,
And tells me a Toothache Tale.

She fills it full of silly words
To jingle in my head, ––
And oh she's glad and <u>oh</u> she's glad,
When she's got me back in bed!

The Bear went over the mountain --

The bear went over the mountain
To see what he could see,
The bear went over the mountain
To find a Christmas tree,
And all he saw was stumps,
And stumps and stumps and stumps,
And one old twisted hickery tree
That seemed to have the mumps.
And all he saw was stumps,

And stumps
and stumps
and stumps.

Of course he had the grumps,
The grumpiest kind of grumps,
For he'd taken his tail and a new tin pail,
And told his wife to forward his mail,
But all he saw was stumps,
In rows and ranks and clumps,
All he found for miles around
Was stumps and stumps and stumps,

And stumps
and stumps
and stumps.

His wife went over the mountain
To see where the bear might be,
His wife went over the mountain
And found a Christmas tree.
She'd taken a knife, like a provident wife,
And she found that Christmas trees were rife
On the other side of the mountain.
Being a provident wife, she knew
Where Christmas trees a-plenty grew,
On the other side of the mountain.

The bear went home from the mountain,
To see what he could see, ––
The bear went home from the mountain
As weary as he could be,
And all he saw was his mother-in-law,
Trimming a Christmas tree.

The Bear went down to the station --

The bear went down to the station
To take the morning train.
The bear went down to the station
And came back home again.
For all he saw was tracks,
And tracks and tracks and tracks,
And a couple of sleepy porters, who
Just grinned and humped their backs.
All he saw was tracks,
And a couple of empty hacks, --
All he found
For miles around
Was tracks and tracks and tracks,
And tracks and tracks and tracks.

Of course he had the blues,
Of deepest, direst hues.
And your belief it should not tax
To hear he had the <u>browns</u> and <u>blacks</u>,
For all he found
For miles around
Was tracks and tracks and tracks,

And tracks
and tracks
and tracks.

Of course he had a fit of blues,
For he'd got up early to black his shoes.
He'd shaken the paw
Of his mother-in-law,
And bought him the latest <u>Traveller's News</u>.
And now it was plain
The choo-choo train
Had left him standing in the rain.
Who <u>wouldn't</u> have the browns and blacks,
When all he saw was tracks and tracks,
When all he spied
Was the rain outside,
And tracks and tracks and tracks,
And tracks and tracks,

    And tracks and tracks
    and tracks and tracks

      and tracks and tracks and tracks?
AND TRACKS!!!

The Bear went down to the market –– or MUTTON STEW

The bear went down to the market
As he had been told to do, ––
The bear went down to the market
To buy some mutton stew,
His wife said: "Bear, I'm telling you,
Now don't forget what you're sent to do.
Buy me a beautiful mutton stew,
And bring it home from the market."

The bear went down to the market
To buy the mutton stew.
He had a car, but he couldn't park it,
For fear that a cop would come and mark it,
While he bought the mutton stew, ––
While he bought the mutton stew.
He had a car, but he scarcely knew
Just what a bear with a car should do
While he went to buy a mutton stew
In the busiest part of the market.
He feared that while he went to pick it,
The cop would leave him a little ticket,
As cops have been known to do, ––
As cops have been known to do.

And while he was thinking it over,
A meddlesome moving-van
Sounded its trump
And came with a bump
That would ruin a weaker man.
And over his eye there rose a lump
As big as a watering can!
"Now what," said the bear, as he found his feet,
"Did they tell me to bring back home to eat?
Was it chops or ham,
Or fish or clam,
Or pickles or syrup or jelly or jam
They said to bring home from the market?
Alas, "He said, as he nursed his eye,
"All I can do is go and try, ––
So I'll see what they have in the market."

Oh he was a worried bear indeed,
As he bought up sausage and caraway seed,
And a peck of peanut butter,
And a side of fancy ham,
Some sneezy pickle,
And some pumpernickel,
And some rhododendron jam.
Then, just to be quite certain,
A quarter of Cheshire cheese.
"It's certainly, certainly," breathed the bear, ––
"Certainly one of these!"

His wife let him in at the kitchen door, ––
When he got back home from the market, ––
Wearing a look he had seen before,
When he got back home from the market.
"Oh Bear, what <u>have</u> you brought us here?"
He murmured meekly, "Everything, dear,
They had down there in the market."

The bear went back to the market,
In the falling summer dew,
The bear went back to the market,
To get the mutton stew.
(For when you forget what you're sent to get,
Well, what else <u>can</u> you do?)
As he stole back home in the twilight,
He scented the scent of ham,
And all he saw
Was his mother-in-law,
Eating the bread and jam.

BUNNYLOGUE

Said the baby to the bunny,
"You are really very funny
With your legs so short and furry,
And your ears so long and limber."
Said the bunny to the baby,
"You may think I'm funny, maybe,
But your legs are funny, very,
Standing tall and round like timber.
And your ears are past explaining, ––
Stubby things that never grew!
While I don't advise complaining, ––
Still, I'd try to order new."
Said the bunny to the baby,
"If you'd make an efort, manybe,
You could pull them just a little
Every day until they're longer.
If at first they're rather brittle,
Exercise wil make them stronger.
They wre worthelsess if they're fragile,
Make them strong and long and agile!"

Said the baby to the buny, "When you say it's I that's funny,
You're a silly, silly rabbit,
And your joking goes too far."
Said the bunny to the baby,
"You're a goosie, you're a gaby, ––
What a silly, silly, silly, silly human thing you are!"

KITTYLOGUE

Said the baby to the kitty,
"You are always sitting pretty
On your window sill so cozy
With the sunshine shining down.
You are always in your corner
Like that lazy boy, Jack Horner,
You don't even stir to take your bath,
Or stroll around the town."

Said the kitty to the baby,
"You my think I'm lazy, maybe,
But you do me great injustice
If you think that I'm a sponger.
I am working for my keep
While the like of you's asleep, ––
And you'd surely be surprised at
All the tricks I have to conjure.
You have dinner set before you,
And a mother bending o'er you, ––
You just have to hold a bottle,
And there's dinner going down!
While I have to catch my victuals
On the hoof, before it skittles, ––
Have to chase the stubborn rodent
To the other side of town.
While your mother waits to feed you,
I must make my way by browsing, ––
Mine's had twenty sets of kittens
Since she set me up in mousing."
Said the kitty to the baby
Twixt a sneezing and a snore.

Said the baby to the kitty,
"You are really rather witty,
But I think that human babies
Have a bigger job to fill."

"Maybe so," admitted kitty,
"For <u>they</u> have to run the city, ––
So just let me go on sleeping
On my sunny window sill."

TEDDYLOGUE

Said the baby to the teddy,
"You are 'most worn out already, ––
What's the use of being gentle
With a bear that's all in pieces?
You're as shapeless as a mutton,
And for eyes, you've just a button,
And you're even leaking sawdust
From you fat a furry creases."

Said the teddy to the baby,
"I'm worn out and feeble, maybe,
But you'd never guess how long ago
I came to live among you.
–– If they ever told you I was new,
I'm forced to say they strung you,"
Said the good old honest teddy
To the naughty, naughty baby.
"I was given to you mother
When she was your age, exactly.
(Around her second birthdy,
If we put it matter-of-factly.)
But the date? I'll never tell it!
It's a secret, –– I'll not sell it,"
Vowed the bear in solumn fashion
With his paw upon his tummy.
"If I told you when she got me,
I'd be telling on your mummy!"

Said the baby to the teddy,
"Your devotion does you credit.
But I'll promise not to spread it,
And you'll tell me smetime, maybe."
Honest Bear'd his answer ready, --
"Silence, oh unworthy baby!
I'd do more to please your mother

Than I would for any other.
She was always kind and gentle
When she wasn't hopping mad.
And for years, I was the favorite
'Mongst the many toys she had."

Said the baby, "Dearest Teddy,
I've been somewhat rough-and-ready,
And I know I've hurt your feelings
When I've romped upon your belt.
But I never'd have begun it,
-- Or not quite so often done it, --
If I'd known before how tender
Were the feeling that you felt.
I'm sure there's not another
Who would do as much for Mother,
And I hope you'll last a long, long time,
The longest that you can.
Oh my sweetest, dearest Teddy," --
(Here his voice became unsteady.)
"Please be careful of you diet
So you'll last till I'm a man!"

RUNAWAY

We had good luck on our walk today,
We saw two fights and a runaway.
One of the fights was cats, the other
A little girl, and her naughty mother.
I don't know quite what the fuss was about,
But it's awful how grown-ups act when out.
–– We ought to be able to find a way
To keep them at home and make them stay.
Just think of the trouble we have about them, ––
Just think of the things we could do without them.
They get in our way and they spoil our fun,
And then they boast about what thay have done!
Just see how my mother behaved today,
When I wanted to watch that runaway.
'Cause I want to go in the street and stand,
She drags me back with a sudden hand, ––
'Cause I want to climb on a butcher's cart,
She holds my fingers so tight they smart!
Silly idea of hers, to stay
On the sidewalk to watch a runaway, ––
Silly idea to hold my hand,
And pick such a stupid place to stand.
These grow-ups should ought to be made to know
We're tired of their trying to run the show!
No matter what anyone else may say,
I know that I'm going to rebel someday!

We had good luck on our walk today, ––
We saw two fights, and a runaway.
We took the air and we bought some bread,
And I've some new notions to put in my head.
And I'm sure that the horse, for some reason or other,
Was trying to get out of sight of his mother!

WAITING FOR THE TRAIN TO GO BY --

When we're going out walking or on our way back,
And we happen to be near the railway track,
We always are hoping, my daddy and I,
We'll be there to see when a train goes by.
> (But Mummy always thinks it's late,
> And stupid just to stand and wait!)

We watch for the light. Is it green, is it red?
Is the train in the station, or coming ahead?
"Now Mummy, be patient, there's nothing to gain
By rushing back home without seeing this train!"
> (Mummy gives a little sigh,
> But she lets us wait till the train goes by.)

"Now Mummy, admit it's a glorious sight. --
That monster all black with his feather of white!"
She smiles <u>so</u> politely. -- I don't see just why,
But we feel a bit guilty, my daddy and I.
> (Mummy waits to be nice, you see,
> But Daddy loves 'em, just like me.)

Woolworth's is the prettiest place
That I have ever seen.
They've piles and piles of peppermints
The most delicious green.
Their player-piano's lovely,
And it always strikes me queer
That Mummy can't be made to come
And get her music here.

And if you think of keeping house,
There's all that you could wish,
Every sort of picture-frame,
And every kind of dish.
When I'm a man, and have become
A millionbillionaire,
I'll furnish all my houses
With the things they sell you there!

CLASSICS

I like the tunes from Carmen 'cause they hop and skip and jump, ––
I like the bass of a Chopin waltz 'cause you work it like a pump.

But the piece I like the best of all was written, it appears,
By a man named Mr. Shoe-man, and it's called, "Two Granite Ears;"

ANN

I do like Ann, ––
She gave me a flower,
She showed me the mill
And the old stone tower,
She took me around
For nearly an hour.
I'll show <u>her</u> something
When I can,
For I <u>do</u> like Ann.

She played with me
On the polished stairs,
We played at sliding,
And running from bears.
She made my hoop
Go 'round so fast,
It looked like train wheels,
Whizzing past.
We played a new
Sort of hide-and-seek,
Till her mother made her
Go study her Greek.
She whispered: "I'll finish it
Quick as i can."
I <u>do</u> like Ann.

She never offers
To hold my hand!
She has the sense
To understand
That personal liberty's
Something grand!
I do like Ann.
We go to her house
Whenever we can.

Mummy likes hers,
But I like Ann.
She talks to me
As man to man.
I do like Ann!

PUSSYWILLOWS

Pussywillow, pussywillow,
Cunning as can be.
Darling little kitty-cats,
Climbing up a tree.
How the furry babies love to have me cuddle them!
Darling little kitty-cats,
Clinging to a stem!

One day in the market, –– I was riding in my cart, ––
I saw my mother look around and give a little start.
"Oh see the pussywillows, the first I've seen this year!
Now I know that winter's gone, and spring is nearly here."

And then she walked along so slow, and hadn't much to say.
And looked as if her thoughts had gone a thousand miles away.
It started folks grumbling 'cause we bumped them in the legs,
And we barely missed the grocer boy, and his basket full of eggs.
When Sister up and asked her what was working in her head,
She smiled a funny little smile, all dreamy-like, and said:
"I'm thinking how I used to go, soon after it was dawn,
To hunt for pussywillows on the hills of Oregon!"

Pussywillow, pussywillow,
Cunning as can be.
Darling little kitty-cats,
Climbing up a tree.
How the furry babies love to have me cuddle them!
Darling little kitty-cats,
Clinging to a stem!
"Cats for sale, cats for sale,
Climbing up a tree!"
Oh Mummy, take your purse and go
And buy them all for me!

YOUNG KING COLE

(Daddy's Version)

Young King Cole was a modern young soul,
A modern young soul was he, ––
He called for his glass and he called for his bowl,
And he called for his Vitamins three.

Vitamin A was a bonny lad,
As clever as he could be.
He could play the fiddle to make you glad, ––
A first class fiddler he!

Vitamin B was an acrobat
Who danced on the edge of the cup, ––
He felt his best when his head lay flat,
And both heels were pointing up.

Vitamin C had a tenor voice
That would melt a sulky stone, ––
He would make the heart of a king rejoice,
When he warbled all alone.

They did their best to amuse the king,
And each with the other vied, ––
But young King Cole was a modern soul,
And he felt dissatisfied.

"Haven't you boys a friend somewhere
Who could pep this music up?"
Vitamin B wore a pensive air
As he perched on the edge of the cup.

"There's a pal of mine who's a jolly boy,"
Said B in a thoughtful tone,
"Perhaps your Majesty'd enjoy
The sound of his saxophone."

So Vitamin D was added to
The fiddlers of the king,
He had the air of something new, ––
And <u>that</u> is a wonderful thing!

But after his charm has worn away,
Ah where will our monarch be?
Will he add to the brethren of Vitamin A
Till he gives us Vitamin Z?

Oh what will he do when the list's gone through,
And they've all in turn been tried?
–– For young King Cole is a modern soul,
And hence, dissatisfied.

BUTTONS

When it's not quite time to go to bed,
But much too late for tag,
Mummy sometimes lets me have
Her saved-up-button bag.

It's fun to sort them out in line,
The big ones and the small,
And there's one old stepped-on button
That's the nicest one of all.

It's much too battered-up to roll,
But it gives me special joy,
For it came off Daddy's uniform
When Daddy was a boy.

I turn it round and round again,
And shut my eyes until
I see a sort of picture
Of my daddy having drill.

I hear the shooting cannons
Making lots of lovely noise,
And see my daddy marching round
With the other college boys.

And thinking of it makes me feel
A little sad, because
I would so love to be a boy
The same time Daddy was!

INHABITANTS

It's a cat or a woman, I don't know which,
But nothing could be unkinder.
> (I'm talking about that wicked witch
> that lives in the coffee grinder.)

He grabs and he snatches whatever he can,
And nothing could be much meaner.
> (I'm talking about that greedy man
> That lives in the vacuum cleaner.)

THE THUNDER--MAKER

There's a great big black dog,
Answer-you-back dog,
That lives up there in the sky.
He barks and howls,
And he snarls and growls,
And he jumps on the clouds piled high,
He's <u>mad</u> 'cause they've tied him up so tight,
And he can't get out of the sky.

He tugs and strains
When it storms and rains,
And he howls when the winds rush by, --
He's having a tantrum away up there,
'Cause they won't let him down from the sky.

When the light'nings flash,
And the thunders crash,
<u>I</u> can tell you exactly why, --
<u>It's that great big black dog,</u>
<u>Answer-you-back dog,</u>
<u>MAD up there in the sky</u>!

VICIOUS CIRCLE

Hurray, we've given the dishes a bath,
Hurray, hurray, hurray!
Oh splashing around in the water's
The best thing in the day!

Hurray, we've given the clothes a bath,
Now <u>that</u> is sport, say I, ––
To soap them good and souse them good,
And hang them out to dry.

Hurray, we've given the floor a bath,
And that's amusing, too, ––
The loveliest, sloshiest, sudsiest thing
Ever a child can do!

Hurray, we're giving me a bath,
And after it's finished, then
The dishes, the clothes and the floor and I
Can start to get dirty again.

SARAH

Mrs. Jones came over to call on Mummy
One afternoon.
I wasn't ready to see her at all, at all.
She came too soon.

Mummy had promised she would take me out. ––
I had to wait.
Mrs. Jones came over much too early,
And stayed too late.

Mrs. Jones told all about her brother's baby, ––
"The <u>sweetest</u> child!"
Mummy sat and smiled <u>so</u> pleasantly,
It drove me wild.

"Dear little Sarah never cries at night, ––
She's always clean, ––
Even when she cut her big back teeth,
She wasn't mean."

"A girl is <u>such</u> a confort after all, ––
A perfect joy, ––
Yes, I know it's very hard to reason
With a boy."

I played in one dark corner with my train,
And turned my back.
I played the train was coming. –– <u>that horrid Sarah</u>
Was on the track.

"And now," I told the engine, "do your worst, ––
Come right ahead!" –– ––
"My little boy would love to see her too,"
My mother said.

I'll bring her over soon," said Mrs. Jones,
"To spend the day."
<u>I'll have some fun with that young Sarah thing
Anyway!</u>

HONEST CONFESSION

Sarah came.
Her eyes were blue.
She had some dimples, --
Quite a few.
Her shoes were very bright and new.
They had a strap, and buckles, too.

When she talked
She lisped a bit.
She held my hand --
I made her quit.
(Of course she didn't make a hit,
But she was't bad, I must admit.)

We ate the candy
That she brought.
We stole some cookies,
And weren't caught.
<u>Next time I'll treat her as I ought,</u>
<u>For I like her better than I thought.</u>

WHY, OH WHY?

Why should he run,
That cat?
Why should he run
Like that?
Just a little fun
From an old pop-gun,
Now, <u>why</u> should he run
Like that?

Why should he jump
Like that?
With his back in a hump,
That cat?
Why should he mind
'Cause I poked him behind
With one little harmless bat?
Now, <u>why</u> should he jump
Like that?

Why should he hide,
That cat?
In his box outside, ––
Like that?
Just 'cause I played
(If he'd only stayed!)
That he was a chair, and <u>sat</u>.
Now, why should he hide
Like that?

Why should he growl
Like that?
Why should he yowl,
That cat?
Just 'cause I held him a little flat,
And covered his head with my grandpa's hat, ––
Now why should he growl
And why should he howl
And why should he act
Like that?
–– Why should he growl,
That cat?

Processional

PROCESSIONAL

There's somebody coming, Mummy,
So put your book away.
Somebody's coming to get a kiss,
And to climb on your lap to stay.
Somebody's coming to see you, Mummy,
So put your book away.

There're two of us coming, Mummy,
To climb up in your chair,
They look oh quite a bit alike,
For they both have curly hair.
Sister is coming to see you too,
So make room in your chair.

There're three of us coming, Mummy,
to give you a nice surprise.
We'll play such a funny, funny game,
If you'll cover up your eyes.
Daddy is coming to see you, too,
That's three in the surprise.

There're four of us coming, Mummy,
So there won't be room in the chair,
There's Sister and then there's Daddy,
And me and the teddy-bear.
So lay every one of those books away,
And put on a cheerful air,
Oh, why should you look
At a stupid book,
When your family is there?

When my mother died in 1984 she left a ring binder of yellowed sheets on which she had typed the poems that she wrote when I was a baby, in the period 1932-34. Among the pages were numerous scraps of paper with drawings that were intended to be included. They were made by G. S. Frasier, a friend of the Family in Paris, who drew them in 1933. The Family returned to the United States soon afterwards and, with the onset of the Second World War, lost all contact with him. None of this material was ever published.

The following two pages are copies of an enclosure in a letter that my grandmother in Portland, Oregon received at Christmas in 1931. My mother had not intended to include them in what she referred to as the "Baby Book" and I am not sure that she ever continued the "diary".

Upon my retirement after many years of university teaching, I recovered the elements of the "Baby Book" and felt that others might enjoy it. I then retyped the poems and copied the original drawings that I found. I have here tried to respect the format of the poems, much as my mother typed them. The layout, as shown, was made by inserting the drawings as I felt she and the artist had intended.

Finally, to fill in the story of the Family, there are in the "Baby Book" numerous references to "Sister". She is Madeleine Turrell Rodack, who now lives in Tucson, Arizona. "Daddy" was of course my father, Charles Alfred Turrell. During the period when the poems were written, he was in the travel business and spent most of the year in New York. He essentially commuted between New York and Paris and thus made 40 trans-Atlantic crossings!

George Turrell
Lille, France
March 15, 2003

NB. As it happens, I am typing this page on my mother's 100th birthday.

I should like to take this oportunity to thank ASA ("l'Association de Solidarité des Anciens de l'Université des Sciences et Technologies de Lille") for its help in the preparation of this little book. The available copies were printed and bound at the "Imprimerie" of the University.

GT

A BABY'S DIARY

Hour by hour.

Six o'clock, and the sunbeams peep,
But my lazy mother is still asleep,
What does she mean by lying there!
I can wake her, - I'll pull her hair!
(It's just the length to pull, you know.
What a pity she's letting it grow!)
Anyway, I can make her yell,
When I've tugged on her raving locks a spell.

I get her up, if she will or no,
At six o'clock in the morning.

Seven o'clock: I've had my food,
I've played with my ball, and I'm feeling good.
I think I'll take a siesta now,
If mother will give me my rubber cow.
Or maybe I'll take the woolly sheep,-
It's just the thing when you're half asleep.
I do get sleepy, I don't know how,
At seven o'clock in the morning.

(But mother's plans are completely foiled,
Her dreams have fled, and her nap is spoiled,
At seven o'clock in the morning!)

Eight o'clock: it is clear and bright,
How nice to wake in the morning light,
And catch the sunbeams as they fall,
Across my bed and on the wall,
(I'm all alone in my little nook.
Sister is studying out of a book.

Mother is fooling around with notes,
Or playing a tune that sweetly floats.

But I am busier than them all,
At eight o'clock in the morning.

For there is my basket, full of toys.
Just the kind that they get for boys.
I have to sort them and set them right,
For they get so mussed up over night.
I like things all neatly piled,
For I am a systematic child.
I like my house all clean and bright,
At eight o'clock in the morning.
Nine o'clock: hey, where's my bath!
I open my mouth and I yell in wrath,
For of all the things that are on my list,
My bath is the one that would most be missed.
Ah, there she comes, and isn't it fun
To hear that glorious water run!
Now I'll go and try my luck
At drowning my fish, and sinking my duck. --
That is the job that is always done
At nine o'clock in the morning.

Bathing Song. (Intermezzo)

Water, water, blesséd water,
How I love your sparkling grace,
How I love to feel you splashing
On my hands and on my face.

How I love to see you moving
When I kick you with my feet,
How delightful to discover,
That my soap is good to eat!

(I'm so fond of pipes and faucets,
That I think I'll be a plumber;
I'll do piping in the winter,
And go swimming in the summer!)

Water, water, naughty water,
You are sometimes very mean,
You are fine to play with babies,
You are cruel to get them clean.

How I love you on my tummy.
How I love you on my rear!
How I hate you on a wash-rag.
How I hate you on my ear!)

       Water, water, sparkling water,
       Every day you bring me joy.
       What a charming, friendly comrade,
       What a playmate for a boy!